AMAZING INVENTIONS

THE ELECTRIC GUITAR

A GRAPHIC HISTORY

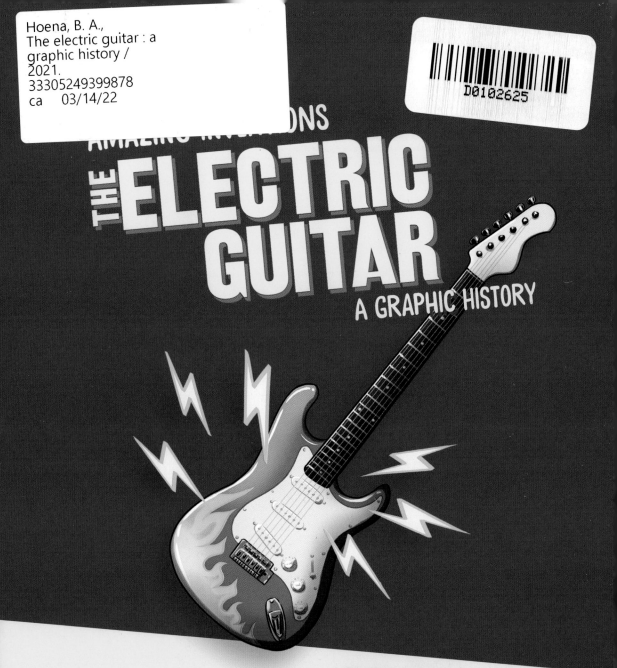

BLAKE HOENA

ILLUSTRATED BY **DAVID M. BUISÁN**

Graphic Universe™ • Minneapolis

Graphic Universe™
An imprint of Lerner Publishing Group, Inc.
241 First Avenue North
Minneapolis, MN 55401 USA

For reading levels and more information, look up this title at www.lernerbooks.com.

Main body text set in CCHedgeBackwards 7/9
Typeface provided by Comicraft.

Library of Congress Cataloging-in-Publication Data

Names: Hoena, B. A. writer. | Buisán, David M., illustrator.
Title: The electric guitar : a graphic history / written by Blake Hoena ; illustrated by David Buisán.
Description: Minneapolis : Graphic Universe, 2021. | Series: Amazing inventions | Includes bibliographical references and index. |
    Audience: Ages 8–12 | Audience: Grades 4–6 | Summary: "For decades, the blasts and howls of the electric guitar have been some
    of the defining sounds of popular music. But more than a century of effort and innovation had to happen before this instrument
    went electric"— Provided by publisher.
Identifiers: LCCN 2020006441 (print) | LCCN 2020006442 (ebook) | ISBN 9781541581470 (library binding) | ISBN 9781728417479
    (ebook)
Subjects: LCSH: Electric guitar—Comic books, strips, etc.—Juvenile literature. | Graphic novels.
Classification: LCC ML1015.G9 H64 2021 (print) | LCC ML1015.G9 (ebook) | DDC 787.87/192—dc23

LC record available at https://lccn.loc.gov/2020006441
LC ebook record available at https://lccn.loc.gov/2020006442

Manufactured in the United States of America
1 - 47330 - 47957 - 2/4/2021

TABLE OF CONTENTS

CHAPTER 1
STRINGS & SOFT SOUNDS

GUITARISTS BRING ALL KINDS OF SOUNDS TO THEIR MUSIC. THEY STRUM A SONG'S RHYTHM. THEY PLUCK CATCHY MELODIES. AND THEY SHRED THROUGH BLISTERING SOLOS.

SHE'S ON FIRE!

YEAH!

WOO-HOO!

BUT THESE ELECTRIFYING INSTRUMENTS WERE NOT ALWAYS CENTER STAGE.

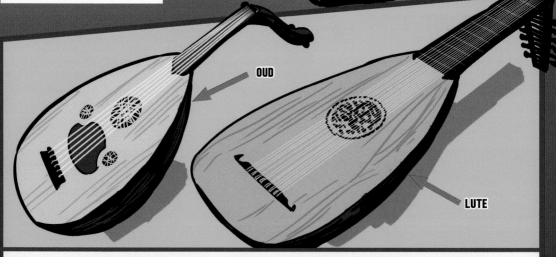

OUD

LUTE

ELECTRIC GUITARS EVOLVED FROM ACOUSTIC GUITARS. AND ACOUSTIC GUITARS EVOLVED OVER THOUSANDS OF YEARS FROM STRINGED INSTRUMENTS LIKE THE OUD AND THE LUTE. THESE ANCIENT INSTRUMENTS HAD HOLLOW, WOODEN BODIES.

SOMETIME BETWEEN THE LATE 1200S AND 1400S, THE GUITARRA LATINA EMERGED IN SPAIN. IT WAS ALSO HOLLOW, BUT IT HAD A BODY THAT NARROWED IN THE MIDDLE. IT ALSO HAD FOUR SETS OF STRINGS. ONE WAS A SINGLE STRING AND OTHER SETS WERE DOUBLE STRINGS.

MANY HISTORIANS CONSIDER THIS INSTRUMENT THE FIRST GUITAR.

OVER THE DECADES, MUSICIANS ALTERED THE GUITAR. BY THE 1600S, A FIFTH SET OF DOUBLE STRINGS WAS ADDED . . .

IN THE MID-1800S, SPANISH INSTRUMENT MAKER ANTONIO DE TORRES JURADO DESIGNED GUITARS THAT WOULD BECOME THE BASIS FOR MODERN ACOUSTIC GUITARS. HIS INSTRUMENT HAD A WIDER BODY, WHICH IMPROVED SOUND QUALITY.

. . . AND A SIXTH IN THE 1700S.

TORRES'S GUITARS ALSO HAD WOUND METAL STRINGS.

AT THE TIME, STRINGS MADE OUT OF ANIMAL INTESTINES WERE COMMON. BUT THESE STRINGS WERE HARD TO KEEP TUNED AND NOT VERY DURABLE. TORRES USED WOUND METAL FOR THE THREE BASS STRINGS. THESE STRINGS WERE STRONGER, AND SOME PEOPLE FELT THEY PRODUCED A BETTER SOUND.

TORRES'S IMPROVEMENTS REVOLUTIONIZED GUITARS. SOON, THE INSTRUMENTS MADE THEIR WAY TO THE UNITED STATES.

STEEL STRINGS GREW POPULAR AMONG AMERICAN MUSICIANS. BUT SIX METAL STRINGS PUT TOO MUCH STRESS ON A GUITAR'S BODY AND COULD CAUSE IT TO CRACK. IN THE MID-1800S, CHRISTIAN FREDERICK MARTIN SET OUT TO FIX THIS PROBLEM.

HMMM . . . I WONDER IF THIS . . .

. . . WOULD PROVIDE BETTER SUPPORT?

HE ADDED AN X-SHAPED BRACE ON THE INSIDE OF THE SOUNDBOARD. THAT INCREASED THE OVERALL STRENGTH OF A GUITAR'S BODY.

AS THE USE OF SIX STEEL STRINGS BECAME MORE COMMON, MORE AND MORE FOLK MUSICIANS PICKED UP THE GUITAR.

OH, GIVE ME A HOME WHERE THE BUFFALO ROAM

WHERE THE DEER AND THE ANTELOPE PLAY

WHERE SELDOM IS HEARD A DISCOURAGING WORD

AND THE SKIES ARE NOT CLOUDY ALL DAY

STEEL STRINGS INSPIRED ANOTHER INNOVATION. IN 1890, US NAVY OFFICER GEORGE BREED MADE AN EARLY ATTEMPT TO COMBINE ELECTRICITY AND GUITARS. HE FILED A PATENT FOR AN ELECTRIFIED VERSION OF THE INSTRUMENT.

IT WORKED DIFFERENTLY THAN OTHER GUITARS. INSTEAD OF PLUCKING OR STRUMMING, PLAYERS PRESSED THE STRINGS TO MAKE SOUNDS! BUT IT WAS NOT ANY LOUDER THAN A NORMAL GUITAR. BREED'S INSTRUMENT DID NOT CATCH ON.

STEEL CONDUCTS ELECTRICITY. WHEN I PRESS DOWN ON A STRING, IT COMPLETES AN ELECTRICAL CIRCUIT, CAUSING THE STRING TO VIBRATE.

IN THE EARLY 1900S, MANY PROFESSIONAL MUSICIANS WERE GROWING FRUSTRATED WITH GUITARS. WHILE THE INSTRUMENTS WERE VERSATILE AND EASY TO PLAY, THEIR VOLUME WAS LIMITED.

OH, WHEN THE SAINTS GO MARCHING IN

OH, WHEN THE SAINTS GO MARCHING IN

I WANT TO BE IN THAT NUMBER

WHEN THE SAINTS GO MARCHING IN

IS THAT GUITARIST EVEN PLAYING?

I CAN'T TELL. I CAN BARELY HEAR HIM.

GUITARS WERE NOT LOUD ENOUGH TO BE HEARD OVER OTHER INSTRUMENTS, ESPECIALLY IN A LARGE ROOM. GUITARISTS WANTED BIGGER SOUNDS.

IN THE 1920s, HAWAIIAN MUSIC WAS POPULAR ACROSS THE UNITED STATES. TO PLAY THIS STYLE OF MUSIC, SOME GUITARISTS LAID THEIR INSTRUMENTS ACROSS THEIR LAPS. THEY USED A STEEL SLIDE RATHER THAN THEIR FINGERS TO HOLD DOWN THE STRINGS.

BECAUSE OF THE STEEL SLIDES, THESE INSTRUMENTS WERE CALLED STEEL GUITARS.

WHILE STEEL GUITARS HAD A UNIQUE, BRIGHT SOUND, THEY DID NOT SOLVE GUITARS' VOLUME PROBLEM. BUT IN THE MID-1920s, STEEL GUITARIST GEORGE BEAUCHAMP VISITED INSTRUMENT MAKER JOHN DOPYERA IN HOPES OF DOING JUST THAT.

WHEN ACOUSTIC GUITAR STRINGS ARE STRUMMED OR PLUCKED, THEIR VIBRATIONS TRAVEL TO THE INSTRUMENT'S SOUNDBOARD. THE SOUNDBOARD PICKS UP THESE VIBRATIONS, AND THE GUITAR'S HOLLOW BODY AMPLIFIES THEM. THE SOUND THEN EXITS THROUGH THE SOUND HOLE.

DOPYERA ADDED RESONATOR CONES TO THE SOUNDBOARD OF BEAUCHAMP'S GUITAR TO FURTHER AMPLIFY VIBRATIONS FROM THE STRINGS.

SOMETIME IN THE MID-1920S, BEAUCHAMP INVITED HAWAIIAN MUSICIAN SOL HOOPII TO TEST THIS RESONATOR GUITAR.

IT WORKS! I CLEARLY HEAR THE GUITAR.

I'VE COME TO SAY GOODBYE . . .

. . . ALTHO' I GO, I'VE GOT THOSE FAREWELL BLUES

RESONATOR CONES HELPED MAKE GUITARS LOUDER, AND RESONATOR GUITARS QUICKLY BECAME POPULAR IN THE UNITED STATES.

CHAPTER 2
AMP UP THE VOLUME!

RESONATORS DID INCREASE A GUITAR'S VOLUME. BUT INSTRUMENT MAKERS WERE NOT DONE SEEKING IMPROVEMENTS TO GUITARS. IN THE 1920S, THEY LOOKED TO A NEW PHENOMENON STREAMING INTO PEOPLE'S HOMES . . .

THE TOY SHOP DOOR IS LOCKED UP TIGHT

AND EVERYTHING IS QUIET FOR THE NIGHT

. . . ELECTRICITY! BY THIS ERA, ELECTRICITY WAS BECOMING COMMON IN HOMES. IT ALLOWED PEOPLE TO USE SMALL APPLIANCES, SUCH AS THE RADIO.

RADIOS CONTAINED VACUUM TUBES, WHICH HELPED TURN RADIO WAVES INTO ELECTRIC SIGNALS.

THESE SIGNALS TRAVELED TO A RADIO'S CONICAL SPEAKERS. THE SPEAKERS THEN TURNED THE SIGNALS INTO SOUND.

AFTER THE SUCCESS OF HIS RESONATOR GUITAR, BEAUCHAMP CONTINUED TO WORK ON MAKING GUITARS EVEN LOUDER.

THIS TECHNOLOGY WOULD HELP INVENTORS FURTHER AMPLIFY SOUND FROM A GUITAR.

IF YOU CAN AMPLIFY RADIO WAVES, WHY NOT AMPLIFY VIBRATION WAVES?

BY THIS TIME, MANY BANDS WERE USING MICROPHONES CONNECTED TO AMPLIFIERS. THESE DEVICES USED THE SAME COMPONENTS AS RADIOS TO BOOST THE SOUNDS OF INSTRUMENTS OR SINGERS' VOICES.

THAT GIVES ME AN IDEA.

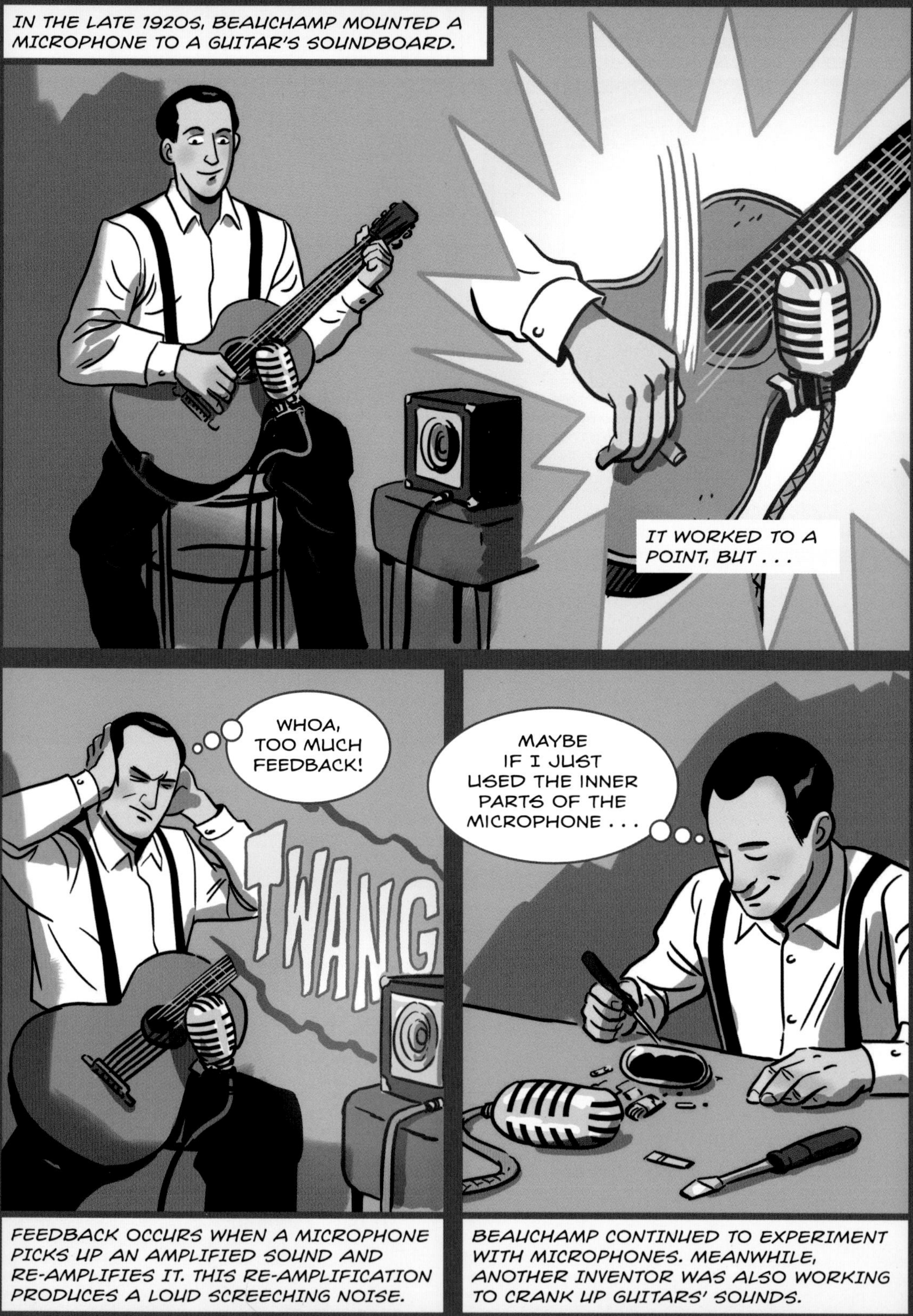
IN THE LATE 1920S, BEAUCHAMP MOUNTED A MICROPHONE TO A GUITAR'S SOUNDBOARD.
IT WORKED TO A POINT, BUT . . .
WHOA, TOO MUCH FEEDBACK!
TWANG
FEEDBACK OCCURS WHEN A MICROPHONE PICKS UP AN AMPLIFIED SOUND AND RE-AMPLIFIES IT. THIS RE-AMPLIFICATION PRODUCES A LOUD SCREECHING NOISE.
MAYBE IF I JUST USED THE INNER PARTS OF THE MICROPHONE . . .
BEAUCHAMP CONTINUED TO EXPERIMENT WITH MICROPHONES. MEANWHILE, ANOTHER INVENTOR WAS ALSO WORKING TO CRANK UP GUITARS' SOUNDS.

ENTREPRENEUR HENRY KAY KUHRMEYER OWNED STROMBERG-VOISINET INSTRUMENT COMPANY. IN 1928, THE COMPANY DEBUTED ITS FIRST ELECTRIC GUITAR.

BELIEVE ME WHEN I SAY, ELECTRIFIED INSTRUMENTS ARE GOING TO BE THE WAY OF THE FUTURE.

THE COMPANY'S ELECTRIC GUITAR WAS CALLED THE ELECTRO. AN ELECTROMAGNET WAS MOUNTED INSIDE THE INSTRUMENT'S BODY. IT PICKED UP VIBRATIONS FROM THE GUITAR'S SOUNDBOARD.

THE ELECTROMAGNET, ALSO KNOWN AS A PICKUP, TURNED THESE VIBRATIONS INTO ELECTRIC SIGNALS. THE ELECTRIC SIGNALS THEN TRAVELED THROUGH A WIRE . . .

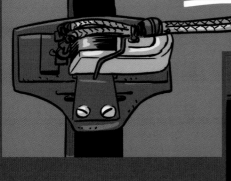

. . . TO AN AMPLIFIER, OR AMP, WHICH TURNED THE SIGNALS BACK INTO SOUND.

WHILE THE ELECTRO WAS LOUDER THAN AN ACOUSTIC GUITAR, THE DIFFERENCE WAS NOT SIGNIFICANT ENOUGH TO MAKE THE INSTRUMENT SUCCESSFUL.

WHILE STROMBERG-VOISINET'S FIRST ELECTRIC GUITAR NEVER TOOK OFF, BEAUCHAMP WAS LOOKING INTO A DIFFERENT APPROACH.

SOMETIME BETWEEN THE LATE 1920S AND EARLY 1930S, BEAUCHAMP MOUNTED A PICKUP FROM A PHONOGRAPH TO A WOODEN BOARD WITH A SINGLE STEEL STRING.

WHAT ABOUT USING A PICKUP TO CAPTURE THE VIBRATIONS FROM THE STRINGS INSTEAD OF FROM THE SOUNDBOARD?

TWANG

THE STRING VIBRATED ABOVE THE PICKUP. THEN, THE PICKUP TRANSLATED THESE VIBRATIONS INTO AN ELECTRIC CURRENT THAT FLOWED TO AN AMP. THE AMP TURNED THE CURRENT BACK INTO SOUND.

TWANG

AS WITH THE ELECTRO, BEAUCHAMP'S EXPERIMENT PROBABLY DID NOT PRODUCE A VERY LOUD NOISE. BUT IT DID PROVE THAT A PICKUP COULD BE USED TO AMPLIFY VIBRATIONS DIRECTLY FROM THE STRINGS OF A GUITAR.

BEAUCHAMP GOT HELP FROM MACHINIST ADOLPH RICKENBACKER AND BUILT A NEW TYPE OF GUITAR. IT HAD A SOLID BODY! BECAUSE BEAUCHAMP WAS FOCUSING ON VIBRATIONS FROM THE STRINGS AND NOT THE GUITAR'S BODY, THE INSTRUMENT DID NOT NEED TO BE HOLLOW.

BEAUCHAMP AND RICKENBACKER CALLED THEIR SOLID-WOOD GUITAR THE FRYING PAN ELECTRIC GUITAR. IT WAS MEANT TO BE PLAYED ON A PERSON'S LAP, LIKE A STEEL GUITAR.

CHAPTER 3
ELECTRIC GUITAR HEROES

BEAUCHAMP, RICKENBACKER, AND OTHERS FORMED THE RO-PAT-IN COMPANY. BY 1932, THEY WERE MANUFACTURING AN UPDATED MODEL OF THE FRYING PAN AND ALSO A HOLLOW-BODY SPANISH-STYLE ELECTRIC GUITAR.

THAT ELECTRIC GUITAR IS AMAZING.

IT SURE IS! IT'S NOT DROWNED OUT BY THE OTHER INSTRUMENTS.

MUSICIAN GAGE BREWER BOUGHT SOME OF RO-PAT-IN'S FIRST GUITARS. IN 1932 ON HALLOWEEN, BREWER PUT ON THE FIRST KNOWN PUBLIC PERFORMANCE TO USE AN ELECTRIC GUITAR. HE PLAYED RO-PAT-IN'S HOLLOW-BODY ELECTRIC GUITAR AS WELL AS A FRYING PAN. HE PLUGGED HIS ELECTRIC GUITARS INTO AN AMP, AND THEY WERE LOUD ENOUGH TO HEAR OVER THE REST OF THE BAND!

A PRESS RELEASE FOR THE SHOW PROMISED "THE WORLD'S NEWEST AND MOST SENSATIONAL INSTRUMENTS."

RO-PAT-IN'S ELECTRIC GUITAR MODELS WERE HITS! BOTH MUSICIANS AND FANS WERE WOWED BY THE AMOUNT OF SOUND THE INSTRUMENTS PRODUCED. BUT MANY PEOPLE THOUGHT THE SOLID BODY OF THE FRYING PAN LOOKED ODD. THE SPANISH STYLE WAS MORE POPULAR. SOON, OTHER AMERICAN INSTRUMENT COMPANIES BEGAN RELEASING THEIR OWN SPANISH-STYLE ELECTRIC GUITARS.

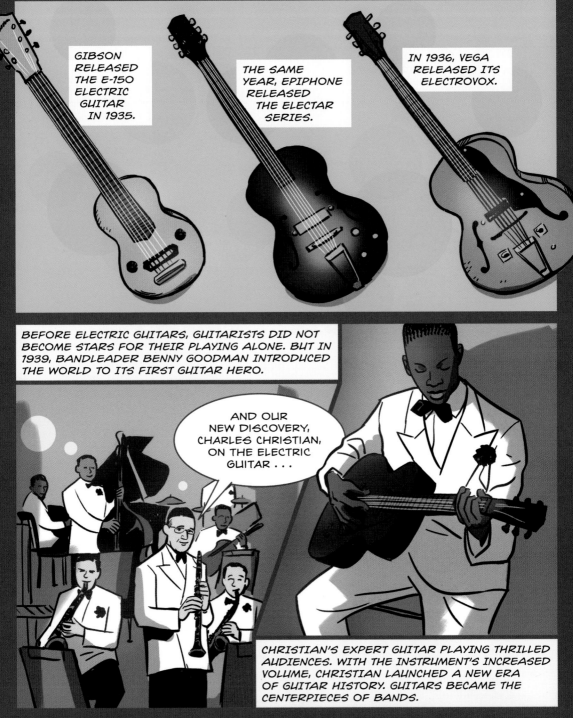

GIBSON RELEASED THE E-150 ELECTRIC GUITAR IN 1935.

THE SAME YEAR, EPIPHONE RELEASED THE ELECTAR SERIES.

IN 1936, VEGA RELEASED ITS ELECTROVOX.

BEFORE ELECTRIC GUITARS, GUITARISTS DID NOT BECOME STARS FOR THEIR PLAYING ALONE. BUT IN 1939, BANDLEADER BENNY GOODMAN INTRODUCED THE WORLD TO ITS FIRST GUITAR HERO.

AND OUR NEW DISCOVERY, CHARLES CHRISTIAN, ON THE ELECTRIC GUITAR . . .

CHRISTIAN'S EXPERT GUITAR PLAYING THRILLED AUDIENCES. WITH THE INSTRUMENT'S INCREASED VOLUME, CHRISTIAN LAUNCHED A NEW ERA OF GUITAR HISTORY. GUITARS BECAME THE CENTERPIECES OF BANDS.

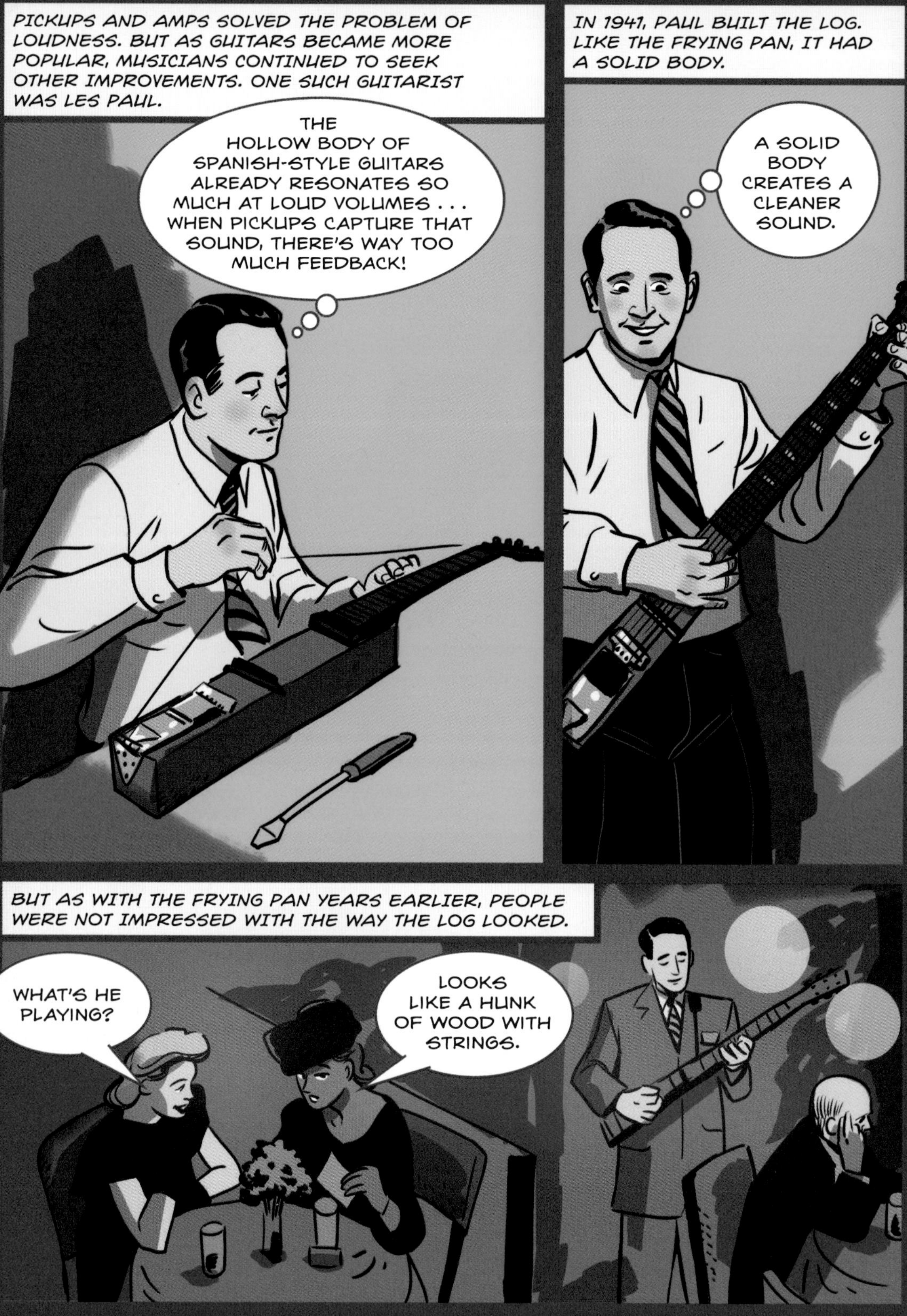
PICKUPS AND AMPS SOLVED THE PROBLEM OF LOUDNESS. BUT AS GUITARS BECAME MORE POPULAR, MUSICIANS CONTINUED TO SEEK OTHER IMPROVEMENTS. ONE SUCH GUITARIST WAS LES PAUL.
THE HOLLOW BODY OF SPANISH-STYLE GUITARS ALREADY RESONATES SO MUCH AT LOUD VOLUMES . . . WHEN PICKUPS CAPTURE THAT SOUND, THERE'S WAY TOO MUCH FEEDBACK!
IN 1941, PAUL BUILT THE LOG. LIKE THE FRYING PAN, IT HAD A SOLID BODY.
A SOLID BODY CREATES A CLEANER SOUND.
BUT AS WITH THE FRYING PAN YEARS EARLIER, PEOPLE WERE NOT IMPRESSED WITH THE WAY THE LOG LOOKED.
WHAT'S HE PLAYING?
LOOKS LIKE A HUNK OF WOOD WITH STRINGS.

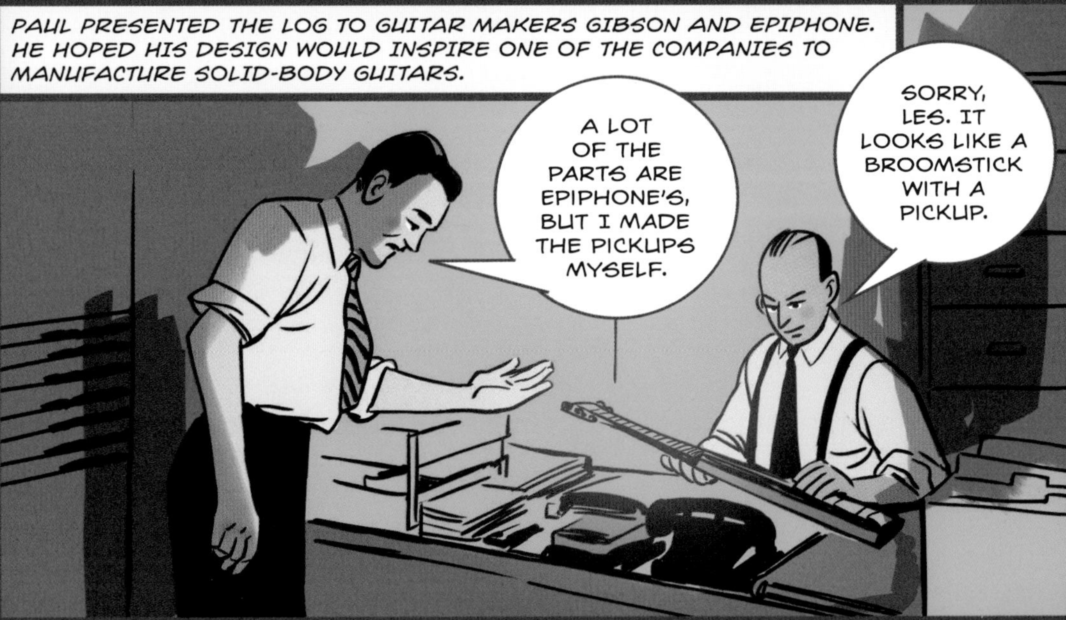
PAUL PRESENTED THE LOG TO GUITAR MAKERS GIBSON AND EPIPHONE. HE HOPED HIS DESIGN WOULD INSPIRE ONE OF THE COMPANIES TO MANUFACTURE SOLID-BODY GUITARS.
A LOT OF THE PARTS ARE EPIPHONE'S, BUT I MADE THE PICKUPS MYSELF.
SORRY, LES. IT LOOKS LIKE A BROOMSTICK WITH A PICKUP.

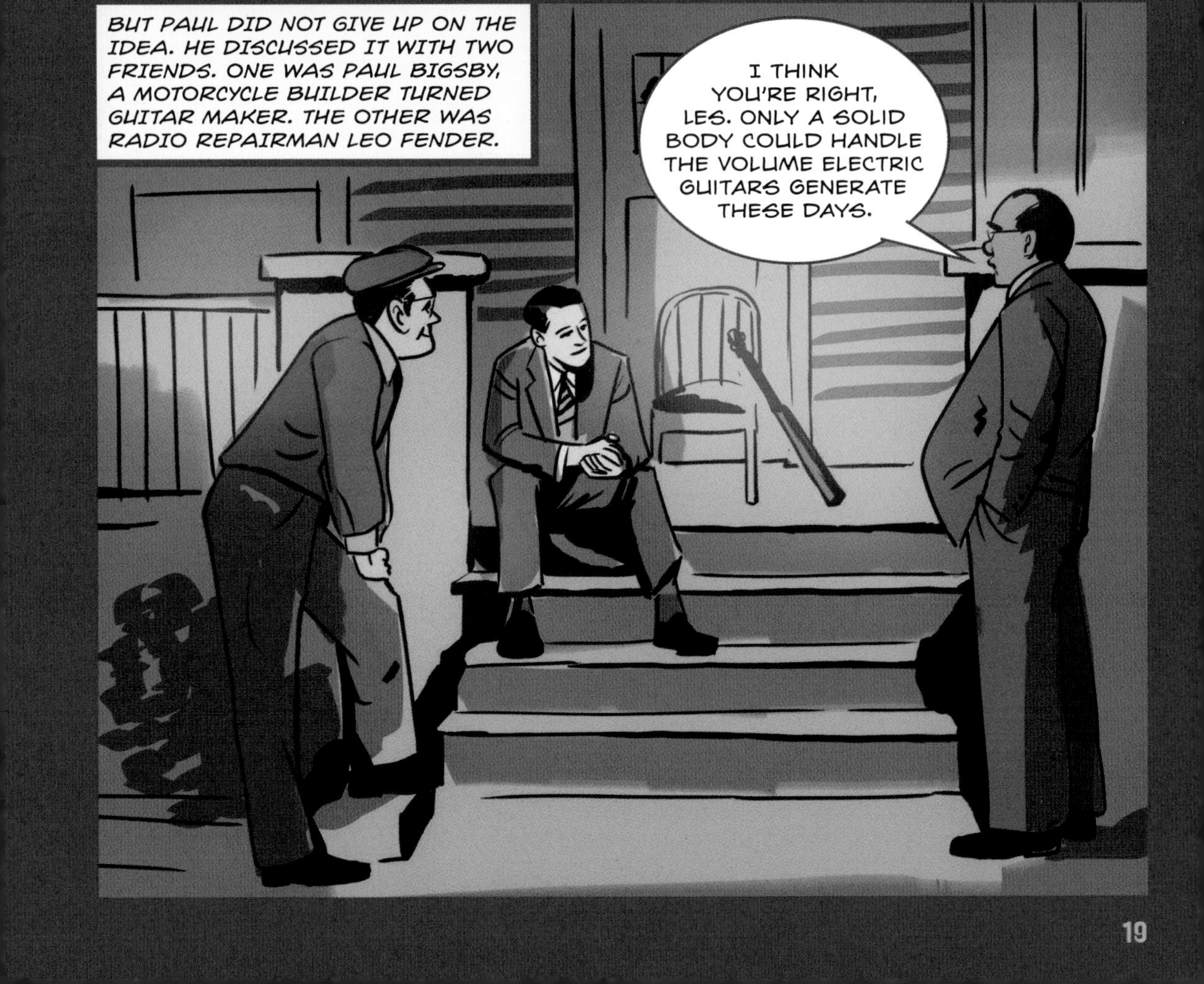
BUT PAUL DID NOT GIVE UP ON THE IDEA. HE DISCUSSED IT WITH TWO FRIENDS. ONE WAS PAUL BIGSBY, A MOTORCYCLE BUILDER TURNED GUITAR MAKER. THE OTHER WAS RADIO REPAIRMAN LEO FENDER.
I THINK YOU'RE RIGHT, LES. ONLY A SOLID BODY COULD HANDLE THE VOLUME ELECTRIC GUITARS GENERATE THESE DAYS.

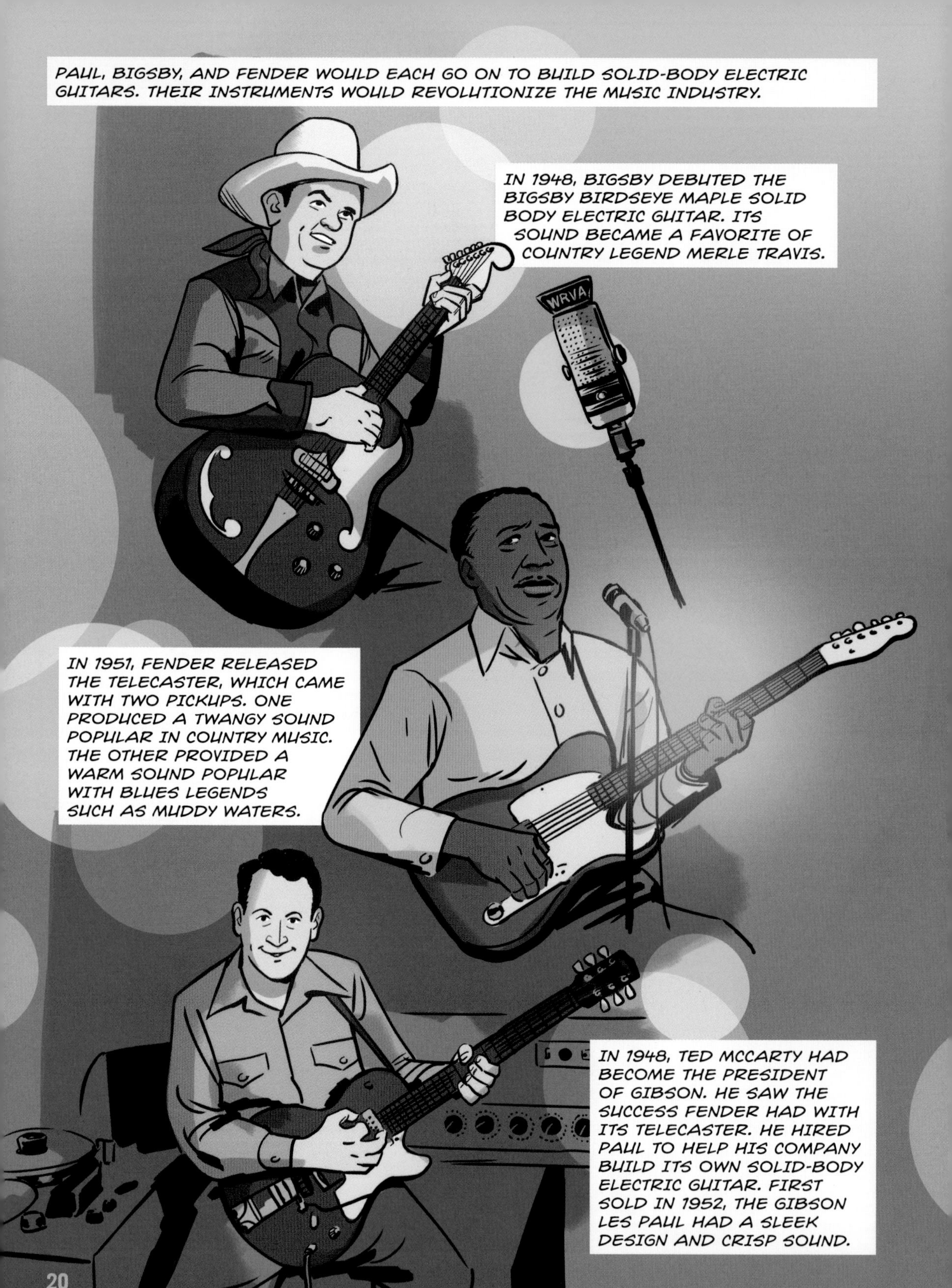
PAUL, BIGSBY, AND FENDER WOULD EACH GO ON TO BUILD SOLID-BODY ELECTRIC GUITARS. THEIR INSTRUMENTS WOULD REVOLUTIONIZE THE MUSIC INDUSTRY.
IN 1948, BIGSBY DEBUTED THE BIGSBY BIRDSEYE MAPLE SOLID BODY ELECTRIC GUITAR. ITS SOUND BECAME A FAVORITE OF COUNTRY LEGEND MERLE TRAVIS.
WRVA
IN 1951, FENDER RELEASED THE TELECASTER, WHICH CAME WITH TWO PICKUPS. ONE PRODUCED A TWANGY SOUND POPULAR IN COUNTRY MUSIC. THE OTHER PROVIDED A WARM SOUND POPULAR WITH BLUES LEGENDS SUCH AS MUDDY WATERS.
IN 1948, TED MCCARTY HAD BECOME THE PRESIDENT OF GIBSON. HE SAW THE SUCCESS FENDER HAD WITH ITS TELECASTER. HE HIRED PAUL TO HELP HIS COMPANY BUILD ITS OWN SOLID-BODY ELECTRIC GUITAR. FIRST SOLD IN 1952, THE GIBSON LES PAUL HAD A SLEEK DESIGN AND CRISP SOUND.

THE SOLID-BODY ELECTRIC GUITAR GREW POPULAR WITH RISING STARS SUCH AS CHUCK BERRY. IT SOON DEFINED A NEW STYLE OF MUSIC THAT EXCITED AUDIENCES LIKE NEVER BEFORE: ROCK 'N' ROLL.

SEVERAL GUITARISTS HAD LAID THE FOUNDATION FOR THIS NEW STYLE OF MUSIC. ONE WAS SISTER ROSETTA THARPE, A GOSPEL MUSICIAN WHO HAD BECOME FAMOUS FOR HER ELECTRIC GUITAR PLAYING IN THE 1940S.

BY THE MID-1950S, THE POPULARITY OF ROCK 'N' ROLL HAD INSPIRED A GENERATION OF YOUTHS TO PICK UP THE GUITAR. BUDDY HOLLY AND HIS FENDER STRATOCASTER ALSO BECAME LEGENDARY.

CHAPTER 4
BEYOND LOUD

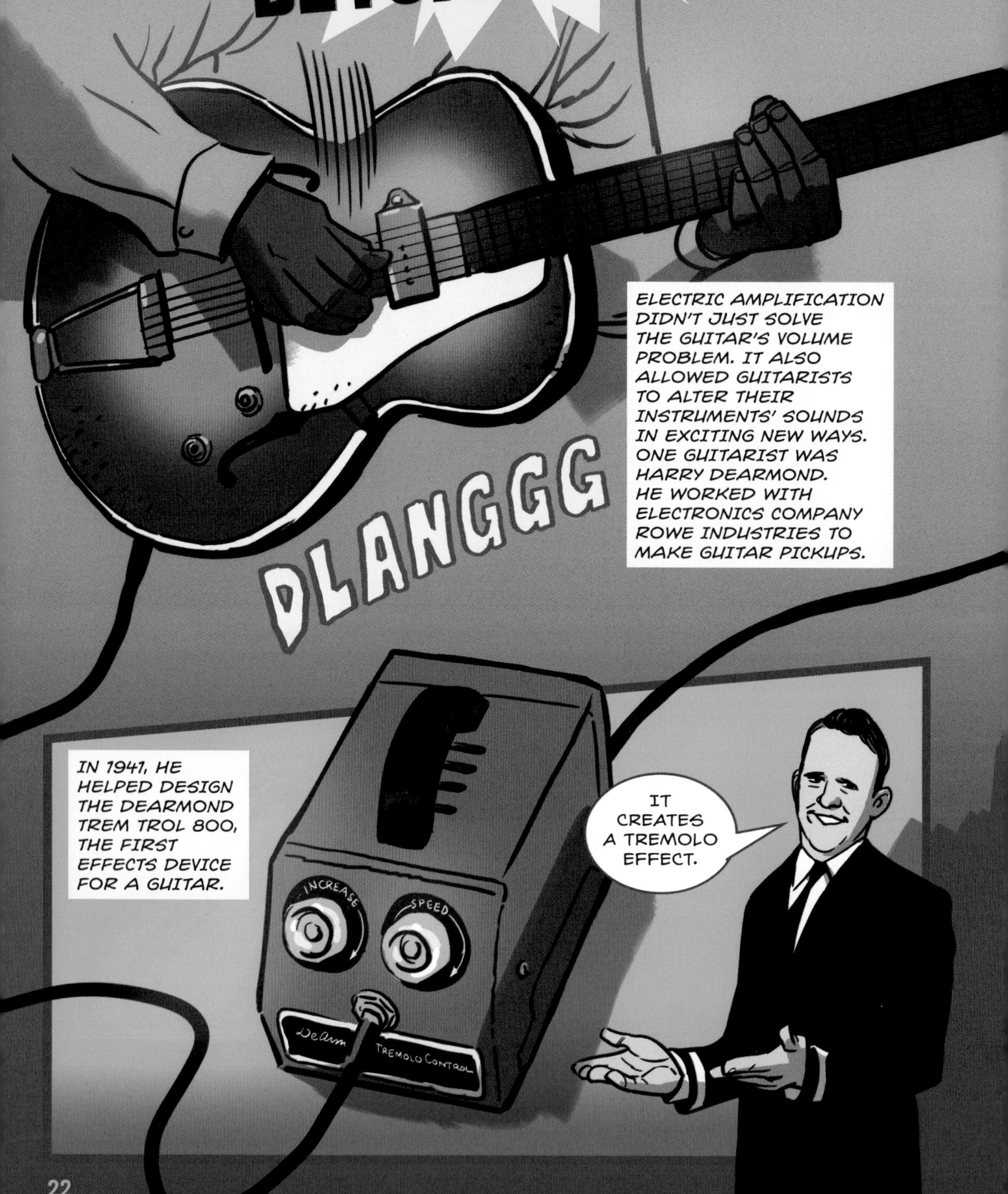
ELECTRIC AMPLIFICATION DIDN'T JUST SOLVE THE GUITAR'S VOLUME PROBLEM. IT ALSO ALLOWED GUITARISTS TO ALTER THEIR INSTRUMENTS' SOUNDS IN EXCITING NEW WAYS. ONE GUITARIST WAS HARRY DEARMOND. HE WORKED WITH ELECTRONICS COMPANY ROWE INDUSTRIES TO MAKE GUITAR PICKUPS.
DLANGGG
IN 1941, HE HELPED DESIGN THE DEARMOND TREM TROL 800, THE FIRST EFFECTS DEVICE FOR A GUITAR.
IT CREATES A TREMOLO EFFECT.
INCREASE
SPEED
TREMOLO CONTROL

WHEN YOU STRUM A CHORD, THE TREM TROL 800 CONTINUOUSLY CHANGES THE VOLUME OF THE SOUND COMING OUT OF AN AMP. THIS CREATES A WAVELIKE SOUND.

TWA WA WA WANG

BLUES MUSICIANS SUCH AS MUDDY WATERS AND BO DIDDLEY MADE THE TREMOLO EFFECT THE CENTER OF THEIR SOUNDS. SOME TREMOLO DEVICES WERE MADE INTO FOOT PEDALS. GUITARISTS COULD TURN THESE DEVICES ON AND OFF BY STEPPING ON THEM.

IN 1962, GIBSON RELEASED THE MAESTRO FZ1-A FUZZ TONE PEDAL. IT GAVE GUITARISTS A NEW, FUZZIER TYPE OF SOUND.

GUITARIST KEITH RICHARDS USED THIS PEDAL IN THE ROLLING STONES' 1965 HIT "(I CAN'T GET NO) SATISFACTION."

CLICK!

REVERB IS ANOTHER POPULAR EFFECT. IT IS A NATURALLY OCCURRING EFFECT CREATED BY THE REPETITION OF SOUNDS, SIMILAR TO AN ECHO.

IN THE EARLY 1960S, FENDER INTRODUCED AMPS THAT CREATED ARTIFICIAL REVERB. THE EFFECT GREW SO POPULAR THAT OTHER COMPANIES BEGAN BUILDING IT INTO AMPS AS WELL.

THIS IS MY FAVORITE SONG!

I LOVE YOU, BRIAN!

BANDS SUCH AS THE BEACH BOYS USED REVERB TO MAKE SURF MUSIC POPULAR.

GUITARISTS ALSO ALTERED ELECTRIC GUITAR SOUNDS IN UNCONVENTIONAL WAYS. DAVE DAVIES PLAYED GUITAR IN THE KINKS. ONE NIGHT IN THE EARLY 1960s, HE USED A RAZOR TO SLASH THE SPEAKERS ON ONE OF HIS AMPS.

HOW IS THIS GOING TO SOUND?

THIS CREATED THE DISTORTED GUITAR SOUNDS OF THE BAND'S FIRST BIG HIT, "YOU REALLY GOT ME," RELEASED IN 1964.

DISTORTED ELECTRIC GUITAR SOUNDS GREW MORE POPULAR INTO THE 1970s. THEY BECAME CENTRAL IN SEVERAL NEW GENRES OF MUSIC, FROM THE PUNK RIFFS OF THE RAMONES . . .

. . . TO THE HEAD-BANGING CHORDS OF METAL BAND AC/DC'S GUITARIST ANGUS YOUNG.

AS INVENTORS AND MUSICIANS WORKED TO MAKE UNIQUE ELECTRIC GUITAR SOUNDS, THEY ALSO EXPERIMENTED WITH THE INSTRUMENT'S DESIGN.

MOST ELECTRIC GUITARS MIMICKED THE SHAPE OF ACOUSTIC GUITARS. BUT THERE WERE POPULAR EXCEPTIONS. ONE WAS THE FLYING V, INTRODUCED BY GIBSON IN 1958. IN THE LATE 1960S, ROCKER JIMI HENDRIX USED THE FLYING V TO PLAY HIS INNOVATIVE SOLOS.

WHY THE FLYING V?

I'M LEFT-HANDED, SO IT WAS EASIER TO FLIP THIS GUITAR AROUND AND PLAY IT.

IN THE 1970S, GUITARIST JIMMY PAGE FAMOUSLY SHOWED OFF A DOUBLE-NECK GUITAR ON STAGE.

ROCK OUT!

26

MUSICIANS SUCH AS EDDIE VAN HALEN REPAINTED THEIR GUITARS FOR A SIGNATURE LOOK. VAN HALEN EVEN COMBINED FENDER AND GIBSON PARTS FOR HIS CUSTOM "FRANKENSTRAT."

EDDIE! EDDIE!

SOME ROCKERS, INCLUDING JOAN JETT, ADDED STICKERS OR OTHER PERSONAL TOUCHES TO THEIR GUITARS.

PLAY "PURPLE RAIN"! "PURPLE RAIN"!

AND BY THE 1980S, ARTISTS SUCH AS PRINCE HAD GUITARS MADE TO REPRESENT THEIR UNIQUE STYLES.

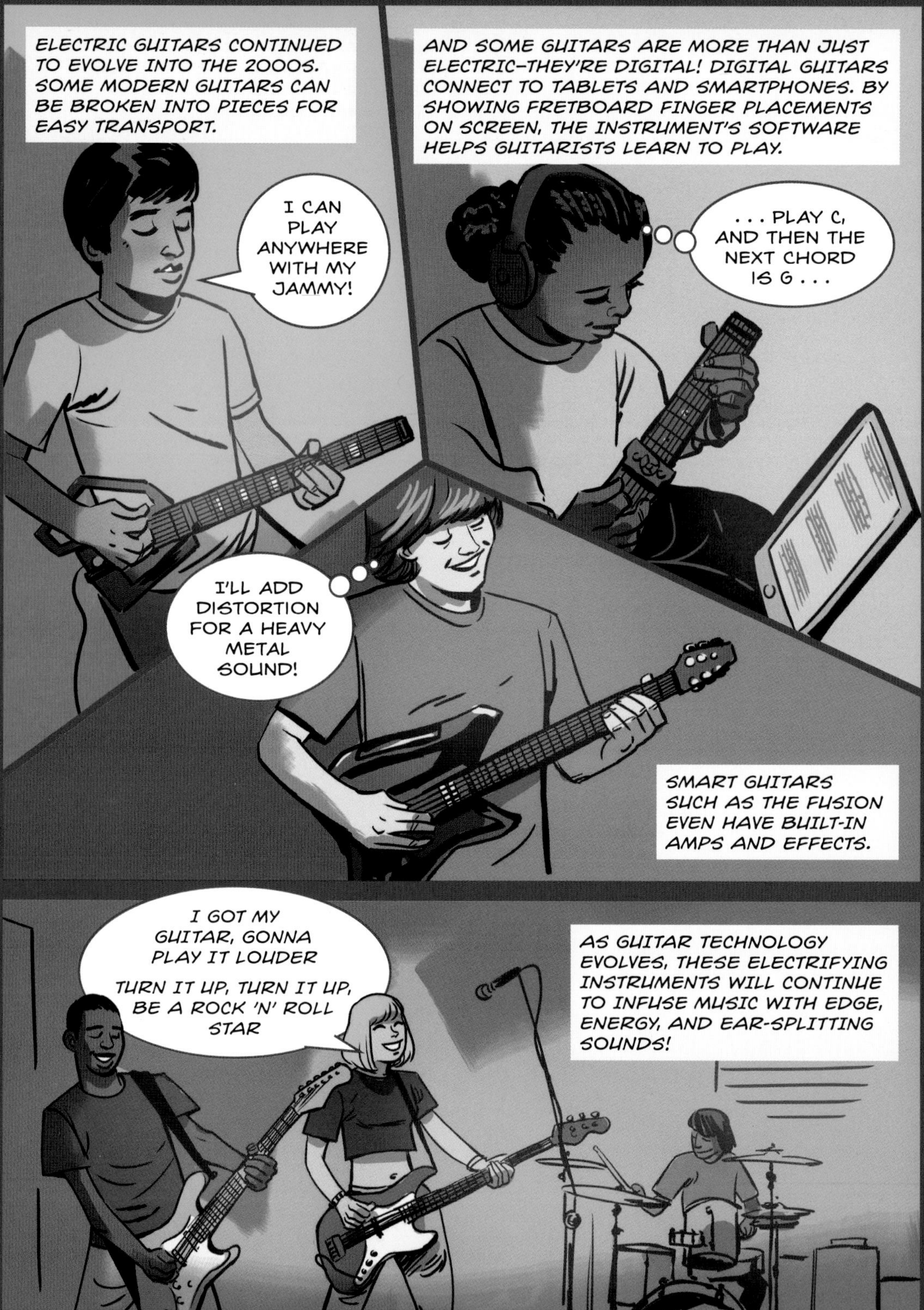
ELECTRIC GUITARS CONTINUED TO EVOLVE INTO THE 2000S. SOME MODERN GUITARS CAN BE BROKEN INTO PIECES FOR EASY TRANSPORT.
I CAN PLAY ANYWHERE WITH MY JAMMY!
AND SOME GUITARS ARE MORE THAN JUST ELECTRIC—THEY'RE DIGITAL! DIGITAL GUITARS CONNECT TO TABLETS AND SMARTPHONES. BY SHOWING FRETBOARD FINGER PLACEMENTS ON SCREEN, THE INSTRUMENT'S SOFTWARE HELPS GUITARISTS LEARN TO PLAY.
. . . PLAY C, AND THEN THE NEXT CHORD IS G . . .
I'LL ADD DISTORTION FOR A HEAVY METAL SOUND!
SMART GUITARS SUCH AS THE FUSION EVEN HAVE BUILT-IN AMPS AND EFFECTS.
I GOT MY GUITAR, GONNA PLAY IT LOUDER
TURN IT UP, TURN IT UP, BE A ROCK 'N' ROLL STAR
AS GUITAR TECHNOLOGY EVOLVES, THESE ELECTRIFYING INSTRUMENTS WILL CONTINUE TO INFUSE MUSIC WITH EDGE, ENERGY, AND EAR-SPLITTING SOUNDS!

SOURCE NOTES

PAGE 6

Song of America: Home on the Range, accessed July 28, 2020, https://songofamerica.net/song/home-on-the-range/.

PAGE 8

Huapala: Waikīkī, accessed July 28, 2020, https://www.huapala.org/Wai/Waikiki.html.

PAGES 10–11, 16

Brad Tolinski, *Play It Loud: An Epic History of the Style, Sound, and Revolution of the Electric Guitar* (New York: Doubleday, 2016) 322, 427.

PAGE 19

"Waukesha County Museum Displays Les Paul's Log," The Les Paul Foundation, December 17, 2014, https://www.lespaulfoundation.org /waukesha-county-museum-displays-les-pauls-log/.

GLOSSARY

ACOUSTIC: relating to any musical instrument that is not electrified

AMPLIFIER: a device that controls the sound from electric instruments

AMPLIFY: to increase, such as the volume of sound

BRACE: a support

DISTORTION: something that alters sound

PATENT: an official document that protects the rights of an inventor's invention

PICKUP: a device that converts string vibrations into electrical signals in the reproduction of sound

RESONATE: to intensify and enrich musical tone by adding vibration. A resonator is a metal device used to achieve this effect.

REVERB: an echo-like sound

SOUNDBOARD: the wooden front part of a guitar's body

TREMOLO: a wavelike sound

VIBRATE: to quiver, tremble, or move to and fro or up and down repeatedly and quickly. This motion is called a vibration.

LEARN MORE

Acousticmusic.org—Timeline of Musical Styles & Guitar History
https://acousticmusic.org/research/history/timeline-of-musical
-styles-guitar-history/

Albertson, Dr. Margaret E. and Emick, Paula. *Music: The Sound of Science*.
North Mankato, MN: Rourke Educational Media, 2019.

Fender—Infographic: Fender through the Years
https://www.fender.com/articles/gear/fender-through
-the-years-a-timeline-of-music-and-instruments

Nabais, Rita. *The History of Rock: For Big Fans and Little Punks*.
Chicago: Triumph Books, 2019.

Rock & Roll Hall of Fame
https://www.rockhall.com/

INDEX